# IN THE HALLS OF VALHALLA FROM ASGARD

## VIKINGS FOR KIDS

### NORSE MYTHOLOGY FOR KIDS
### 3RD GRADE SOCIAL STUDIES

MW00582140

**BABY PROFESSOR**
EDUCATION KIDS

Speedy Publishing LLC

40 E. Main St. #1156

Newark, DE 19711

www.speedypublishing.com

Copyright 2017

All Rights reserved. No part of this book may be reproduced or used in any way or form or by any means whether electronic or mechanical, this means that you cannot record or photocopy any material ideas or tips that are provided in this book.

In this book, we're going to talk all about Norse mythology. So, let's get right to it!

Before the Vikings were converted to Christianity, they believed in pagan gods. These gods were the Norse gods, which means the "gods of the north." Like the gods of ancient Greece and Rome, the Norse gods had the same faults as ordinary human beings do.

NORSE GODS-WARRIORS

They sometimes were very jealous or had temper tantrums. They weren't immortal as the Greek and Roman gods were thought to be, but they lived longer than normal human beings and they also had magical superpowers.

Some historians believe that the Vikings adapted some of the ancient Greek myths as their own. The ancient Greeks,

who worshipped gods they believed lived on Mount Olympus, lived ten centuries before the Vikings.

ODIN

# WHERE DID THE NORSE GODS LIVE?

he Vikings believed that their gods lived way up in the heavens in a place described as Asgard. The palaces of the Norse gods were constructed with elaborate decorations of gold as well as silver. The most elaborate of all the palaces was the one belonging to Odin, who was the leader of all the Norse gods. Odin's palace was called Valhalla.

# THE HALLS OF VALHALLA

The Viking warriors believed that if they were courageous and died in battle, they would awake in Odin's palace. There they would be welcomed as heroes and enjoy sumptuous banquets in the company of the mighty god Odin. When a warrior passed away, he was sometimes cremated with his favorite possessions so that he would quickly cross over into the halls of Valhalla.

Sometimes, a dead Viking chief would be placed on his favorite boat so it could be burned or buried with him. In that way, when he got to Valhalla, he would be able to travel on his boat again.

# HOW DID THE VIKINGS WORSHIP THEIR GODS?

**A**rchaeologists don't know as much as they would like to know regarding how the Vikings paid homage to their Norse gods. They think it's possible that the Vikings had wooden buildings or shrines to their gods since there are many tales concerning trees with magical powers. As far as historians know, they didn't have specific religious leaders or standard ceremonies.

VIKING WARRIOR

Instead, most of the knowledge regarding their gods was passed down in stories, which they loved to tell. The Vikings all knew the different myths and told them from generation to generation. The mighty god Odin was revered by warriors and kings. Newborns were given a charm blessed by Thor, the god of thunder, to protect them.

# WHO LIVED IN MIDDLE EARTH?

**T**he Vikings thought of the universe as an enormous tree. This world tree was called Yggdrasil. There were nine different domains at different levels of the tree and its roots went down to the underworld. Midgard, also called Middle Earth, was one of the nine domains and humans lived there with other creatures. Midgard was formed when Odin and his two brothers, named Vili and Ve, killed Ymir, who was a giant.

YGGDRASIL

T he Norse gods were able to see all the other creatures that lived in Midgard, but almost all of these creatures were invisible to human beings. There were immense giants who controlled storms, frost, and ice. There were also scary goblins and hideous monsters. Mischievous elves and dwarfs lived there too.

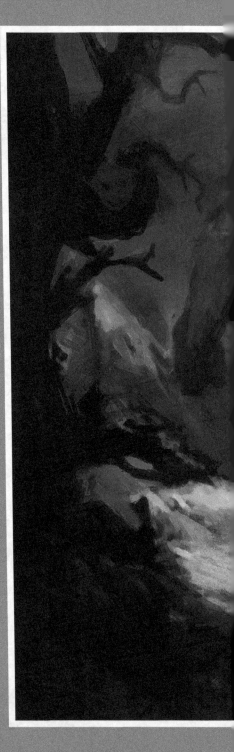

**T**he gods were always having dangerous encounters with the creatures of Midgard, especially the many giants. However, even though the giants were very powerful, the Vikings didn't worry about the fate of their gods, because they knew that their gods were very clever. They also knew that their gods had an advantage since they could always escape to their homes in Asgard if they needed to.

HEIMDALL

# HOW WERE MIDDLE EARTH AND ASGARD CONNECTED?

**M**idgard and Asgard were connected with a huge rainbow bridge, which was called Bifrost. There was a god whose job it was to protect this bridge and his name was Heimdall. Heimdall had amazing, magical powers of vision and hearing.

**H**e could see someone coming from more than 100 miles in the distance whether it was day or night. His hearing was so excellent that he could hear the sounds made by growing grass! As you can imagine, hardly anyone got past Heimdall if they were trying to sneak into Asgard.

ASGARD

# THE MYTH OF ODIN AND HIS RAVENS

din was the ruler of all the Norse gods, but he was known for many other qualities as well. He was the god of poetry and the god of wine. He was also the god of war and of knowledge. Sometimes he was called the Raven god because he had two ravens that sat on his shoulders. One raven was called Huginn, which means "thought" and the other was called Muninn, which means "mind."

Every day his loyal ravens flew around the Viking domains and reported on all the happenings of humans, giants, and other creatures. Thanks to his ravens, Odin was

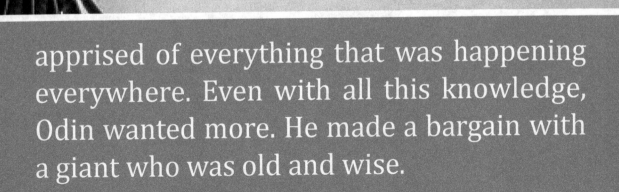

apprised of everything that was happening everywhere. Even with all this knowledge, Odin wanted more. He made a bargain with a giant who was old and wise.

**H**e gave up one of his eyes so that he would have all the world's wisdom. The giant took Odin's eye and gave him all the wisdom he wanted. This is why depictions of Odin's early life show him with two eyes, but later he is shown with a patch over his missing eye.

# WHO WAS THOR?

Odin had a son and his name was Thor. Thor was the god of thunderstorms and strength. He had lots of magical tools including a belt, a hammer, gloves made of iron, and a chariot. Thor had two goats to pull his chariot through the sky. One was named Toothnasher and the other was named Toothgrinder.

THOR'S HAMMER

LOKI

# WHO WAS LOKI?

Odin had another son too. His adopted son's name was Loki and he was mischievous. He shows up in lots of different Norse myths because he's a shape shifter, which means he can transform himself into different animals or people. He loved to play jokes on people, but sometimes his jokes caused destruction or death.

# THE TALE OF BALDUR

There was once a Norse god who was so good that he appeared to give off light. His name was Baldur. He was Thor's brother and the son of Odin and Frigga. Unfortunately, Baldur began to have horrible nightmares that someone was trying to kill him. He asked his mother, Frigga, for help because she was a powerful goddess. She was able to cast a magical spell so that no matter what anyone tried to throw at Baldur, nothing would get through to him.

BALDUR

The other Norse gods found it amusing that Baldur couldn't be hurt. They began to throw spears, axes, arrows, and rocks at him but they just

bounced off. Baldur found it startling to have an ax thrown at his face, but he knew Frigga had protected him so he didn't complain.

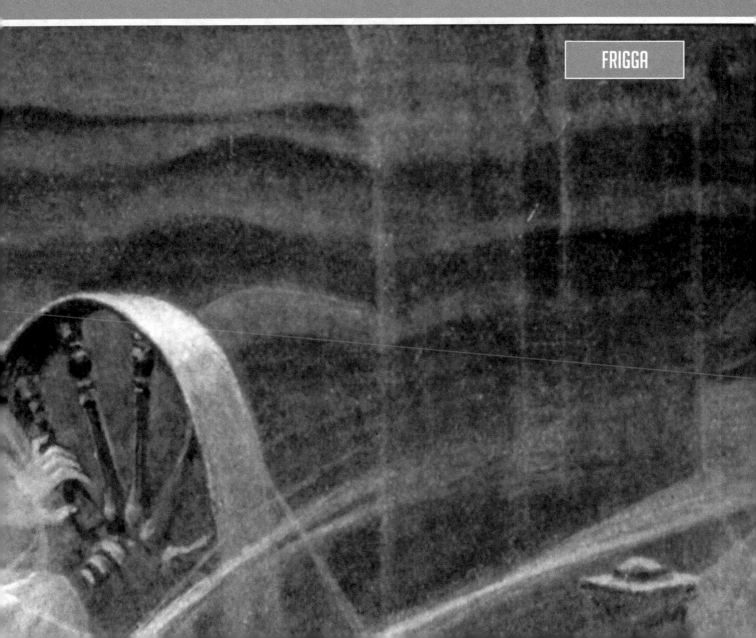

FRIGGA

L oki was so tired of hearing about Baldur and how great he was. He transformed himself into an old woman so Frigga wouldn't know who he was, then he complimented her on her spell. All the flattery went to Frigga's head so when Loki in the guise of the old woman asked, "Did you leave out anything?" Frigga answered.

Haudr hin blindi. legg hi i Gleipnis
Balldur hin Odba brodur sin me
teini Ept til vijsan Loba laufeij
Las XLII Dæmi Sogu Eddu bo

**S**he confided in the old woman who was really Loki and told her, "I left mistletoe out. Mistletoe is such a tiny twig, I didn't think it could cause any harm." That's exactly the information that Loki needed. Loki sharpened a mistletoe twig in preparation. Then, he found an old god who was nearly blind and wanted to throw something at Baldur for fun.

Loki guided the old god's hand so the twig could be thrown at Baldur with superhuman force. The twig went right through Baldur's heart and killed him instantly. The other gods were shocked at what had happened. Loki acted shocked too, but of course everything had gone according to his plan. He was so glad to get rid of Baldur, the annoying do-gooder.

SIF

# THE STORY OF SIF

**S**if was the harvest goddess and she had long locks of beautiful blond hair the color of wheat. One day the prankster Loki snipped off most of her hair. Sif was so terribly sad that her salty tears flooded Midgard and the crops began to die.

**L**oki was afraid that Sif's husband, Thor, would give him an angry beating when he found out. Loki requested that the dwarfs spin some new golden hair for Sif. They did, so Loki avoided trouble and Sif had her beautiful hair once again.

# WHEN THE VIKINGS BECAME CHRISTIANS

A s they migrated to other countries in Europe, such as Britain and Germany, some Vikings became Christians. They adopted Christian ways and built churches in honor of Christ and used decorative crosses. However, some Vikings continued to worship the Norse gods.

others blended their old myths with their new Christian beliefs. The older warriors who believed they would see the halls of Valhalla in Asgard were the last to give up the ancient mythology.

# SUMMARY

One thousand years after the ancient Greeks worshipped their gods who lived on Mount Olympus, the Vikings told stories of their Norse gods who lived in Asgard. Their gods had human weaknesses, but they had superhuman powers. Archaeologists don't know if the Vikings had standard rituals for the worship of their gods, but the Vikings loved the stories of the Norse gods and passed them down from generation to generation.

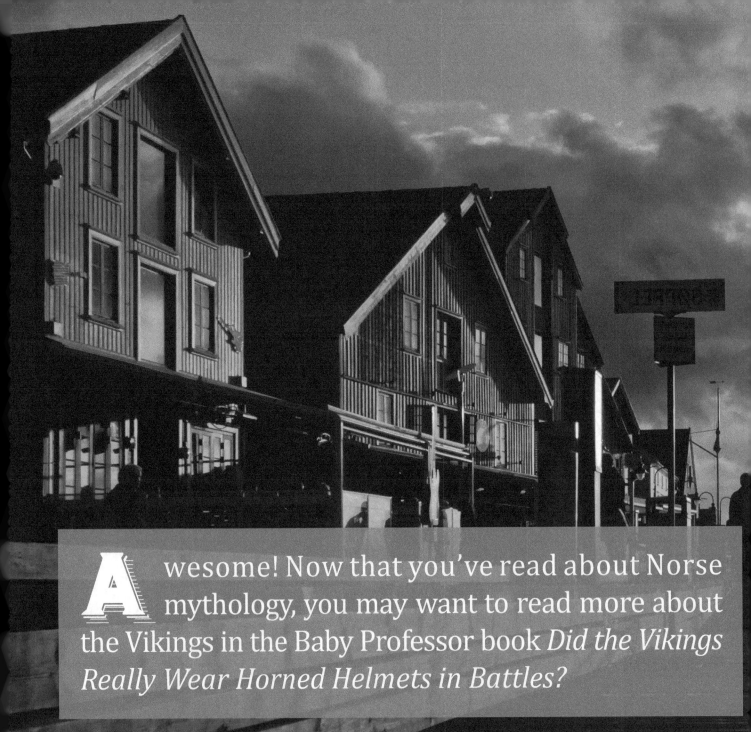

**A**wesome! Now that you've read about Norse mythology, you may want to read more about the Vikings in the Baby Professor book *Did the Vikings Really Wear Horned Helmets in Battles?*

Visit

**BABY PROFESSOR**
EDUCATION KIDS

www.BabyProfessorBooks.com

to download Free Baby Professor eBooks
and view our catalog of new and exciting
Children's Books

CPSIA information can be obtained
at www.ICGtesting.com
Printed in the USA
LVHW061733040220
645815LV00008B/486

9 781541 917354